NARRATIVE ON COMMUNALISM IN INDIA

VOLUME 1, ISSUE 4 OF BRILLOPEDIA

ANURAG DHABARDE

ISBN 979-888546356-0

Contents

Preface

"Start writing, no matter what. The water does not flow until the faucet is turned on".

-Louis L'Amour

Hundreds of students and professors are contributing their work to Brillopedia, we are here to provide ample information about Law and Contemporary issues. Our aim is to provide a platform for today's generation to express their views and ideas on law and contemporary law.

Publication

This research paper is published in volume 1, issue 4 of Brillopedia

CHAPTER ONE

ABSTRACT

It is broadly agreed that the spectre of developing communalism is the maximum vital trouble going through India today. In the war for the soul of Indian nationalism 3 positions were staked out. Firstly, there are folks that insist that Indian nationalism ought to relaxation on cultural and mental foundations of an impeccably Hindu provenance, though the ecumenical man or woman of Hinduism licenses pragmatic shifts in interpretation for you to deflect prices of communalism. Secondly, there are folks that insist that Indian nationalism ought to derive from secular principles. Notwithstanding the iconic problems of unique definition, the term 'secular' does own an agreed center meaning: country neutrality in regards to faith. In a multireligious society like that of India, this will imply both an essential separation of the country from spiritual pastime and affiliation, or country impartiality on all problems regarding the spiritual hobbies of various communities. In practice, 'Indian secularism' has been a combination of the two: an unsatisfactory try to reconcile what a few recalls to be basically incompatible approaches. A narrower area of operation, restricted for the maximum element to educational as opposed to activist or famous debate. Nevertheless, it's been claiming more and more adherents. It holds that due to the fact secularism is in starting place a profoundly Western, or as a minimum unIndian, concept, it's far intrinsically at odds with the truth of non-Western/non-Christian life in general, and with Indian genius in particular. What is for that reason known as for isn't always secularism, nor Hindu nationalism, however an anti-secularism which opposes factitious tries at isolating faith from politics and as an alternative encourages using the 'authentic' sources of religion to create a sociopolitical lifestyle with a greater deep-rooted and authentic tolerance of range and pluralism than 'Western secularism' can ever generate. Religion itself is to be the important thing aid withinside the warfare in opposition to communalism. State-concentrated theories of the way to engineer the social good (the present-day secular country) are themselves the problem, the stimulus in the back of communalism; to that ought to be counterposed the sources of a religiously suffused and religiously plural civil society. Basically, Here Indian anti-secularism can to a degree be part of forces with post- modernist celebrations of difference, range and pluralism, likewise positioned in civil society and threatened via way of means of the technocratic country. These competing claims offer the context for the subsequent reflections on communalism and nationalism, and their putative not unusual place ground. In order to combat communalism, we ought to be sure that we recognize what it's far and the way it grows. To combat it withinside the call of an earthly nationalism calls for us to recognize nationalism as well, to recognize precisely what it stocks and does now no longer percentage with communalism. Some tries at definition are consequently actually in order.

Keywords - Anti- secularism, Communalism, Indian secularism, Multireligious society, Sociopolitical lifestyle, Western secularism

INTRODUCTION

The concept of communalism is a product of the religion that is the roots of this practice lies in the belief of religion. Basically, the people who are willingly involved and are also the followers of a particular ethnic group. It is basically a strong attachment of one person to his own culture and community which they certainly try to flaunt in front of other communities and make other population understand that their community is superior and better than other available communities. But, the attachment towards their community is/can be considered unhealthy in Indian context. It's an ideology that, in order to unify the community, suppresses distinctions within the community and emphasizes the essential unity of the community against other communities[1]. In Indian context, the definition and explanation of communalism may be different and vast from other regions as India is the only country where there are people with many beliefs and this might be a concrete reason behind the emergence of communalism in India. Division in the beliefs of people does not lead to this but the people who are in majority, the community with large beliefs try to influence the thoughts and make them understand, forcibly the importance and superiority. With this approach towards religion, ethics or any random community, a big difference and diversities in thoughts, their choices (people) can be observed. A factor for the rise of communalism in India was in the 19th Century, when several religious organizations were formed by the Hindu and Muslim communities whose goals were poles apart. These were organizations that began to play communal politics in their favor. This belief is fundamentally flawed. People of one religion do not have the same interests and aspirations in every context. Everyone has several other roles, positions and identities. There are many voices inside every community. All these voices have a right to be heard. Therefore, any attempt to bring all followers of one religion together in context other than religion is bound to

suppress many voices within that community
[1] communalism

CHAPTER THREE

ROOTS OF COMMUNALISM IN INDIA

In the reign of Britishers rule in India, the 'Divide and Rule' strategy worked in Favour of the Hindus at first. Because as the British deposed the Muslim rulers, they naturally looked at their enemies' Muslims and supported the Hindus as an opponent to them. But they came to be considered as a serious threat to the stability of British rule with the growth of political ideas and national consciousness among the Hindus, and the government realized the need to put a check on this risk. The Muslims had not abandoned their truculent attitude toward the British and had not yet established the national spirit that the Hindus had imbued with half a century of Western education.[1] Communalism as a political philosophy has its roots withinside the spiritual and cultural range of India. It has been used as a political propaganda device to create divide, variations and tensions among the groups on the idea of spiritual and ethnic identification main to communal hatred and violence. In historical Indian society, humans of various religion coexisted peacefully. Buddha changed into possibly the primary Indian prophet who gave the idea of secularism. Meanwhile, Kings like Ashoka observed a coverage of peace and spiritual tolerance. Medieval India witnessed the appearance of Islam in India marked with the aid of using occasional occurrences of violence along with Mahmud Ghazni's destruction of Hindu temples and Mahmud of Ghor's assault on Hindus, Jains and Buddhists

During the latter half of the 19th century, there was a shift in British policy regarding their approach towards Muslims. The British sought support from the Muslims in order to influence Hindus with the advent of a nationalist spirit among the Hindus. At this juncture, it was the Muslims that They were also able, under the leadership of Syed Ahmad, to put implicit confidence and in the government's benevolence. The appeal of Syed Ahmad to the British government to take the Muslims under their purview, thereby finding a ready response and achieving to a far greater degree than he could ever hope for. In the eighties and nineties of the nineteenth century the government's strategy of favoring Muslims as an opponent against the Hindus became increasingly clear. This basically talks about how Britishers approach towards religion in order to acquire power and how different communities can be used to remain in power. It particularly explains that powers can be politically acquired with the help of different communities. There are mainly 2 different segments of communalism which are dominant in the Indian situations which are elaborated particularly as follows:

- Political
- Social

Although, all these two segments are interlinked to each other and partially dependent on each other, helps each other to be described and are also based on the concept of religion.

[1] 601.pdf

CHAPTER FOUR

SOCIAL COMMUNALISM

It is the department of communalism that's in particular depicting the societal conditions concerning how communal misery is created an on what foundation The communal violence that stony-broke get into Surat in the aftermath of the demolition of the Babri musjid which definitely came about in 2002, near Godhra Station, a teach educate become set ablaze and fifty-eight people have been singed alive. The hearthplace befell withinside the repercussions of a rivalry among sellers, Muslims and Hindu-proper activists, getting back from Ayodhya. While the real motive for the hearthplace is puzzled and people successful nonetheless cannot appear to be dealt with, the episode become applied to plant scorn and brutality towards Muslims withinside the city groups, cities, cities and ancestral areas of north and focal Gujarat. The public authority and nation hardware got here out with numerous legitimizations for the butchery, thinking about it a "unconstrained response." Their vocal assist introduced great crowds onto the roads without precedent for Gujarat's lengthy records of collective savagery. For a clearly lengthy time, geared up crowds of hundreds assaulted, plundered and fed on houses, shops, laaris (pushcarts), lodges, and manufacturing traces claimed via way of means of Muslims. In extra of 100,000 people misplaced their houses and approach for vocation. Something like 2,000 people misplaced their lives and equal numbers have been all of the whilst lacking 12 months after the episode. A part of the vernacular-language press assumed a component in inducing the savagery, whilst memories approximately the attack of Hindu girls have been applied to legitimize ruthless rapes on Muslim girls. Numerous Muslim girls have been stripped, assaulted or bodily afflicted in complete standard visibility. A few have been scorched alive to annihilate the evidence of attack. It is past the world of opportunities to count on to decide the real wide variety of girls who faced sexual savagery seeing that even in ordinary situations girls enjoy problems saying such encounters. In this unique setting, it become extraordinarily tough for them to file the viciousness as the ones successful acted with none capacity repercussions. A few girls' activists and truth gazing organizations recorded records approximately the encounters of girls. Something like three hundred such episodes had been recorded from specific portions of Gujarat. the severity and heinous effects outline the discrimination with a whole hatred towards one unique network sincerely on the premise at the religion. 1992 foreshadowed the incidents that have been to arise anywhere Gujarat in 2002. The seen participation of Hindu ladies withinside the violence become decided withinside the Surat riots. despite the fact that there had been a few instances wherein ladies supported and reclaimed ladies of various groups as part of their preference on the fee in their very own security, the majority of women recognized with and acted on behalf in their very own spiritual network. In those riots, Muslim ladies have been raped, mutilated, paraded bare and burnt alive, but there has been a blackout in the media regarding the brutality of the violence towards them. This blackout displays 2 principal issues related to the growing strength of communal and fundamentalist forces publicly lifestyles and politics. First, that communal ideology is closely pervasive withinside the way of thinking of maximum journalists and editors of the vernacular press, and second, that the danger of bodily attack via way of means of fundamentalist forces, and their felony impunity, is extensive understood. the method moreover the} several media of dissemination have been additionally carefully thought of with the intention to attain definitely specific strata, as the bulk were not tuned in to the scale, depth and brutality of the occasions due to the partial media coverage. we generally tend to prepared many meetings at the college subject for academics and students, to expose commonness with survivors and to obtain people's dedication to the problems. With a memo addressed to the residence Ministry and additionally the National Women's Commission, we generally tend to carried out an in-intensity signature marketing campaign hard-to-please justice and rehabilitation for sufferers in Vadodara and on the country wide level. These efforts succeeded in pressuring the National Women's Commission to visit Surat. generally, tend to discovered a two-web page leaflet to talk ladies' reviews of sexual atrocities, and prepared a avenue play to shake the sensibility of the Hindu majority and bring our feminist knowledge of the occasions. The play, "Aapane tolu Bani Gaya chhe" (We have become a Crowd), introduced out the plight of survivors via way of means of depiction real occasions symbolically and with only some words, mistreatment entirely quick talk and songs. The message for the majority network become that we generally tend to hardly ever observe the effect of our movements while appearing at some point of a crowd. which generally tend to may or may not immediately take part in violence on some other network, but in a crowd, form of a herd of sheep, we purposely or by accident help those who act violence or spread the ideology of violence. we generally tend to try to conceal our crime towards humanity in the obscurity of a crowd, and therein approach we generally tend to moreover lose our humanness. For girls, the message become that in case you keep silent regarding atrocities devoted towards ladies from specific groups, subsequent time, it might be your turn. better than all, it is important to uphold our identification as ladies and as human beings, in place of as individuals of one or some other spiritual network.

CHAPTER FIVE

SECULARISM

Communalism turned into and remains one of the main demanding situations to democracy in our country. The makers of our Constitution have been aware about this challenge. That is why they selected the version of a mundane country. There isn't any respectable faith for the Indian country. Unlike the reputation of Buddhism in Sri Lanka, that of Islam in Pakistan and that of Christianity in England, our Constitution does now no longer provide a unique reputation to any faith. The Constitution presents to all people and groups freedom to profess, exercise and propagate any faith, or now no longer to observe any4. The Hindu nationalist each misunderstands and knows the character of nationalism. He or she is inaccurate to peer nationalism as a herbal entity. Since the state is a 'collective country of thoughts striving to emerge as a political fact', it possesses an inherent fluidity which makes it able to loss of life out, of metamorphosing, of status on a number of cultural foundations. The historic debate on the character of Indian culture—whether or not it is largely Hindu, whether or not it's far viable to set up the basically Hindu, whether or not it's far religiously composited each stand other than Indian nationalism and is importantly connected to it. It is hooked up due to the fact a experience of countrywide identification is built in component from competing interpretations of the uncooked materials of history. It stands aside due to the fact Indian nationalism isn't always 'logically' built out of a few perceptions of 'accurate' history. This isn't always a modern fruit of any specific cultural-historic logic, nor does it certainly relaxation on a few cultural-historic 'essence' rooted withinside the beyond and enduring via the ages. Indian nationalism isn't always certainly Hindu nationalism; nor, incidentally, is it certainly a composite or secular nationalism. It can be suited to relaxation it on compo web page cultural foundations which additionally have their personal traditions; however, this is something else.

Secular nationalism, or at the least the absence of a Hindu nationalist political order, does now no longer derive its legitimacy from History or the beyond however from its promise, now no longer from origins as a whole lot as from its suited effects. A social order that's to be steadily humanist and democratic can't concurrently be Hindu nationalist or communally founded. This is enough to outline the legitimacy of secularism. Indian nationalism is something whose cultural-emotional content material should be fought for. Here the Hindu nationalist knows complete properly his or her task. To make the case for Hindu nationalism per- suasive, people and agencies have released a veritable onslaught on the cultural, ideological, social and political levels, in general from their positions in civil society. Part of this onslaught entails recourse to a scientific distortion of history, to the dogmatization and territorialization of Hinduism. This should correctly be defined as its tried Somatization centering Hinduism on unique texts, gods and goddesses, locations of worship, myths, symbols, and so forth, which can be to be made pre-eminent and broadly mentioned as such. To the volume that that is viable it serves psychologically to 'unify' the numerous Hindu network in a manner which the Hindu nationalist hopes will extensively lessen the relevance of different identities like class, gender and caste. For those identities can shape the idea for mobilization round needs which erode this team spirit and provide ability for corporation throughout spiritual divides

CONCLUSION/SUGGESTION

Communalism is acidified communitarianism. It sees itself as enemies locked in a permanent war with one another. It certainly indicates that there must be differences in the choice of religions and that it is supposedly responsible for generating hatred between communities of different kinds. The Indian citizen should be against communalism, can be seen as a necessity of the moment when the current situation speaks of chaos, but nobody should condemn the legitimate forms of communitarianism. It is simply a mistake to fuse communitarianism with communalism. Understood in this sense, secularism is not just an ideology of some parties or people, this idea is one of the foundations of our country, communalism should not be seen as a threat to some people in India, it threatens the idea of India itself, so it must be Being communalism A secular constitution like ours is necessary but not sufficient to combat communalism. Prejudice and propaganda in the community must be counteracted in everyday life and in the politics of religious mobilization.